ESSENTIAL
CHILDREN'S
ROOMS

TERENCE CONRAN

ESSENTIAL CHILDREN'S ROOMS

THE BACK TO BASICS GUIDE TO HOME DESIGN, DECORATION & FURNISHING

305515213

A

Contents

14

Planning & Design

44

Furniture & Fittings

76

Décor & Detail

INTRODUCTION

PLANNING & DESIGN

FURNITURE & FITTINGS

DÉCOR & DETAIL

Introduction

Creating successful children's rooms means thinking about both the detail and the big picture. Detail, because you will need to meet very specific requirements at specific times in a child's life to cope with the demands of each developmental milestone; and the big picture, because the arrival of children means that you will have to consider the space at your disposal as a whole. A family home is not just a home with a child's room in it; it enshrines a completely different way of living, as all new parents quickly discover. Particularly critical in this respect is achieving the right balance between shared and private space.

Starting a family is a key turning point in anyone's life and for many people it is at this stage that they are most likely to move from a small flat or apartment to a larger home. Moving, however, is not always possible each time you increase your family. Other strategies may well have to come into play, such as reallocating or altering space to suit your changing needs, or taking a step further and extending or converting your home in order to free up additional room. Inevitably it also entails a radical rethink of storage provision. There is no escaping the fact that you are going to need twice as much storage space before very long.

LEFT: A SUSPENDED POCKETED TIDY KEEPS TREASURES AND TOYS ON VIEW, WHILE A WINDOW SEAT MAKES A COSY PLACE TO CURL UP WITH A BOOK.

ABOVE: INCLUDING AN EATING AREA IN THE KITCHEN CREATES AN EASY LIVING SPACE WHERE THE FAMILY CAN COME TOGETHER THROUGHOUT THE DAY.

continued

Introduction

For many parents, the arrival of a new baby understandably brings out the nesting instinct, and decorating and equipping a nursery for a newborn is a natural expression of this. It is important to bear in mind, however, that children are emerging personalities in their own right and quite early on will begin to develop preferences of their own. This is not to say that you should let your child dictate how you decorate and furnish their room, or give in to pester-power as soon as it manifests itself, rather that you should not do all the imagining on their behalf. Themed children's rooms are big business and they can be fun for a while, provided your child is engaged with the theme. But whether it takes the form of a relentlessly coordinated nursery scheme smothered in ducks and bunnies, or what amounts to an indoor adventure playground for junior pirates, the themed room often says more about adults than it ought to. More important is to allow a child scope to put their own stamp on their surroundings. You only need to consider the way certain toys are one-hit wonders, while other more open-ended playthings can spark hours of invention and make-believe. If you keep the basic surfaces and finishes of your child's room relatively plain there is space for their imagination to take flight.

Most people can remember their childhood rooms in great detail in later years and this is not surprising. A child's room is their very first experience of personal space and fosters their growing sense of individuality and territory. While it needs to be flexible enough to accommodate new stages of development, it should also provide a sense of continuity through years of rapid change, in other words, psychological security. This is just as true where siblings are sharing a room.

Security, of course, also means safety. It is difficult to anticipate every potential hazard, but all first-time parents need to spend a little time thinking about how to adapt their home to create a more risk-free environment for the new family member. It is important to choose furniture, equipment and furnishings for children that have been designed and constructed to conform to the highest safety standards.

ABOVE: A COSY BUILT-IN BOX BED INCORPORATES STORAGE DRAWERS AND SHELVES, LEAVING SPACE IN THE REST OF THE ROOM FOR THE BABY'S CRIB.

RIGHT: THIS STURDY SMALL-SCALE TABLE IS IDEAL FOR CREATIVE ACTIVITIES. CHILDREN ALSO NEED PLENTY OF FLOOR SPACE TO PLAY ON.

INTRODUCTION

PLANNING & DESIGN

FURNITURE & FITTINGS

DÉCOR & DETAIL

Basic considerations

Children grow fast. Being able to anticipate what is coming next will help you plan more effectively and stay ahead of the game. In many cases this means building in flexibility as far as possible.

- A key early issue is room allocation. This may be a fairly straightforward choice when your first child is on the way as a new baby requires relatively little room; later when a sibling arrives you may well need to rethink space and swap bedrooms around. The same is true when children reach the teenage years.
- Consider how well shared spaces, such as living areas and kitchens, serve the functions of your family life.

- Take every opportunity to build in additional storage space.
- Bathrooms are often bottlenecks in the family home. Is there scope for enlarging an existing one or adding a second or third?
- Think about childproofing. This is not simply a question of safety, but also peace of mind. In the early years, it is important to accept that precious, breakable items should be stored or kept well out of reach.
- As far as possible, try not to schedule any major improvements or alterations to your home in the weeks leading up to the birth of your child in order to avoid the stress of an unnecessary deadline.

ABOVE: IN THIS SHARED BEDROOM FOR TWO LITTLE GIRLS, A SIMPLE DECORATIVE SCHEME AND WHITE PAINTED FURNITURE ENHANCE THE SENSE OF SPACE.

RIGHT: STORAGE CONCEALED BEHIND SEAMLESS WHITE PANELS IS A PRACTICAL AND UNOBTRUSIVE SOLUTION FOR COPING WITH THE CLUTTER OF FAMILY LIFE.

Ages & stages

Babies

For many parents-to-be, furnishing and decorating a nursery is a natural expression of the nesting instinct. Others prefer to acquire only the bare minimum until after the newborn has arrived.

Until a routine begins to establish itself, all you really need in terms of specialist furniture and equipment is somewhere for the baby to sleep, a changing mat and a limited amount of storage space for clothes, toys and supplies such as nappies and other baby products. Depending on your parenting style, it is often a good idea if the first bed is a portable basket or cot, which allows you to keep the baby close by you, both during the day and at night-time. Later on, when a sleep pattern emerges, you can move the baby to a proper cot and a room of their own.

Babies are far from blank slates. More important at this stage than a roomful of nursery furniture are toys that stimulate early conceptual development. Playthings that are brightly coloured or patterned, musical or mobile will all provide fascinating entertainment. A supported seat or bouncer that gives a baby a better vantage point on the intriguing new world around them will also be very useful.

LEFT: IN THE EARLY MONTHS, BABIES CAN FIT IN WITH THE FAMILY AND DO NOT NEED MASSIVE AMOUNTS OF SPECIALIST FURNITURE OR EQUIPMENT.

ABOVE: A SIMPLE CHEST OF DRAWERS IS A VERSATILE INVESTMENT AND CAN BE USED TO STORE NAPPIES, SPARE LINEN AND BABY PRODUCTS IN THE EARLY MONTHS.

Continued

Ages & stages

Early years

The first word, the first tottering steps, the first temper tantrum – the early years are marked by a number of developmental milestones that arrive in quick succession. Now is the time to give serious thought to childproofing your entire home, if you have not done so already.

Toddlers and pre-schoolers learn through play and by investigating the world around them, often messily and sometimes destructively. A good deal of that play takes place at floor level and a warm, resilient surface is more comfortable and provides better sound insulation than a hard or unyielding one. Other finishes need to be robust and easy to clean.

As possessions accumulate, you will have to pay greater attention to storage. Simple modular containers, where you can organize like with like at low level, make good sense and allow your child easy access to their toys and belongings. At this stage, out of sight is out of mind, while toys and games on high shelves only tempt children to risky feats of climbing.

By the age of three, most children are ready to move into a proper bed. Some make the transition more easily than others. You can help to allay fears or anxieties by providing the reassurance of a nightlight, which is also useful if your child has to get up and pay a visit to the bathroom after bedtime.

LEFT: A BED WITH INBUILT STORAGE FREES UP FLOOR SPACE IN THIS SNUG BEDROOM.

RIGHT: THIS RED RACING CAR MAKES BEDTIMES EXCITING AND THE MULTI-STRIPED CARPET CREATES A COLOURFUL AND COMFORTABLE PLAY AREA.

Continued

Ages & stages

School-age

The school years dramatically widen a child's perspective. During this stage, when the greater portion of the waking hours is spent in a classroom, a child's room assumes even greater importance as a private retreat. At the same time it must often serve as a shared space too, when friends come to play, or when another sibling comes along. Accommodating these different functions, as well as ensuring each child has a sense of their own territory, means building in a degree of flexibility.

Multipurpose furniture such as bunk beds, platform beds with study areas slotted underneath and modular storage can all help to make the most of available space and keep the floor area as clear as possible. Storage is a major challenge. School-age children rapidly develop new interests and activities, but may not yet be ready to say goodbye to old toys, books and games. Periodic clearouts and good negotiating skills are essential.

Within reason, it is also important to acknowledge your child's emerging likes and dislikes by allowing them some say when it comes to decoration and furnishing. Soft furnishings, such as curtains or bedding, that are relatively easy and economical to change, can provide the vehicle for expressions of loyalty, whether it is to a football team or a favourite cartoon character.

ABOVE: A MODULAR STORAGE UNIT DOUBLES UP AS A BEDSIDE TABLE. ACCESSORIES SUCH AS THIS MIFFY CHARACTER CLOCK ARE EASY TO CHANGE AT A LATER DATE.

LEFT: WHEN OLDER CHILDREN ARE SHARING, BUNK BEDS OR PLATFORM BEDS ARE OFTEN A GOOD SOLUTION, ALLOWING STUDY AREAS AND ADDITIONAL STORAGE TO BE BUILT IN UNDERNEATH.

Continued

Ages & stages

Teenagers

When your child approaches puberty, chances are you will need to rethink how space is allocated, especially where siblings have been sharing. Most teenagers will be prepared to put up with a relatively restricted area if that means they can shut the door on the rest of the household. Separate rooms not only give teenagers privacy and autonomy, they serve as useful cooling off zones during what can be fairly tempestuous years.

As a parent, your job is to make sure that the basic framework is in place: that there is a well-lit study area to encourage good working habits, enough storage space for clothes and belongings, and a bed that offers enough support for a 'child' who now may well be the same height and weight as you are. Aside from that, it is a good idea to take a back seat and allow your teenager the freedom to customize their bedroom to their own taste. At some point, most go through a collaging phase, which might not be to your liking, but there are more important battles to be won.

If noise is an issue, it can be a good idea to convert part of your home into a dedicated teen area to create a place for computer games, band practice, or where friends can hang out.

ABOVE: ALL-WHITE MODERN FURNITURE AND A MONOCHROME DAISY PRINT WALLPAPER CREATE A SOPHISTICATED BEDROOM FOR A TEENAGE GIRL.

RIGHT: A BLUE-GREEN COLOUR SCHEME MAKES A STRONG STATEMENT IN A BOY'S BEDROOM. A GOOD WORKING AREA IS ESSENTIAL FOR TEENAGERS.

Spacial strategies

Room allocation

The first decision to make about a child's room is which one is it going to be? Most homes offer at least some scope for choice. While initially it may seem sensible to allocate smaller bedrooms to children and the largest to the adults, the size of the occupants is not the real issue: activity is. Adults chiefly use their bedrooms for sleeping and relaxing, whereas children's rooms are more multifunctional.

When children are small they need a lot of floor space to romp about and play. If that floor space is not available in their own room, they will find it in the kitchen or the living area, which may not be what you want. Allocating the largest or 'master' bedroom to children, particularly if two siblings are sharing, can help to ease pressure on the entire household. Switching bedrooms around involves no expense and does not take much time or effort.

The next time you may wish to review matters is when a child reaches their teenage years. Teenagers have a greater need for wall area on which to plaster statements of identity rather than floor space for building castles, and most do not mind having a small bedroom if it means that they get it to themselves.

ABOVE: GIVING YOUNGER CHILDREN THE LARGEST BEDROOM CAN HELP KEEP THEIR CLUTTER CONTAINED IN ONE LOCATION.

LEFT: A LARGE, HIGH-CEILINGED SPACE SERVES AS A SHARED BEDROOM FOR TWO BROTHERS AND OFFERS PLENTY OF ROOM FOR A TABLE FOOTBALL GAME.

Continued

Spacial strategies

Opening up

One of the key issues involved in planning a family home is getting the balance right between shared or communal areas and private spaces. While fully open layouts, such as converted lofts, often prove impractical once children come along, it is still a good idea for main living areas to be as inclusive as possible. Spatial alterations that remove dividing walls will not directly increase floor area, but they will promote a sense of spaciousness that can be beneficial.

The difficulty and expense of the work will depend on whether or not the wall or walls you intend to remove are structural or not. Partition walls, which do not play a structural role, can be taken down with no further intervention. If you remove a structural wall, however, you must put a compensating element back in place, generally in the form of a steel beam or joist.

Options

■ Removing a wall between a kitchen and dining room to create a family kitchen.

■ Removing partition walls between hallways and living areas.

■ Knocking two small rooms into one to create a family bathroom, larger living area or a large shared bedroom.

■ Enlarging the access to the back garden to blur the boundary between indoors and out.

ABOVE: SHARED SPACES COME IN ALL SHAPES AND FORMS. HERE AN EXTRA-LONG SOFA PROVIDES ROOM FOR THE WHOLE FAMILY TO SNUGGLE UP TOGETHER.

RIGHT: AN OPEN-PLAN KITCHEN AND EATING AREA INCLUDES A SEPARATE AREA TO ONE SIDE WHERE CHILDREN CAN PLAY UNDER SUPERVISION.

Continued

Spacial strategies

Partitioning

By the time the teenage years loom on the horizon you may well find that children who have been happily sharing a bedroom up until now would prefer their own private space. Partitioning a large room, either flexibly or permanently, can win you the additional bedroom that is required without having to go to the expense and disruption of building a full-scale extension to your home.

- When you are partitioning a large room, the new dividing wall must be sited so that there is at least one window in each of the two new rooms that you create. By law, all spaces described as 'habitable', which includes bedrooms, must have a window.
- Think about how to arrange the layout so that each bedroom can be separately accessed.
- Partition walls can be very simply and economically constructed out of plasterboard over a studwork frame. They are not structural and they do not impose significant loads on the existing floor, which makes the work very straightforward.
- An alternative to a permanent divider is some form of flexible partition, such as a screen that concertinas back on itself, or sliding or bifolding doors. This allows you to keep your options open, partitioning the spaces by night and connecting them by day.

ABOVE AND LEFT: IN THIS CONVERTED ATTIC SPACE CENTRALLY POSITIONED STAIRS CREATE A NATURAL DIVISION BETWEEN TWO BEDROOMS. CHILDREN LIKE QUIRKY SPACES AND THE PORTHOLE-STYLE WINDOWS CREATE A DEN-LIKE FEEL.

Continued

Spacial strategies

Mezzanine levels

Dividing up space vertically, rather than horizontally, can be another useful strategy in children's rooms. A proper mezzanine level, where the upper level serves as an additional floor, requires a double-height area. But a high-level sleeping platform can work equally well and can be constructed in a bedroom where the ceiling is a normal height.

- Unless you have a double-height space to work with, plan the siting of the platform or upper level so that your child can at least sit up in bed without banging their head.
- Decide how extensive you want the platform to be. It should be at least the size of a single mattress for comfortable sleeping. Too large, however, and you will begin to affect the usefulness of the rest of the room.
- Creating a mezzanine, where the load of the new level is supported by existing walls, is structural work. Building up a platform from floor level is more straightforward.
- Think about how you will use the space underneath the platform: for study, storage, or as a play area?
- Safe access is key. The means by which the platform is reached, whether it is a ladder, metal rungs, or any other form of steps, needs to be robust and securely anchored.

ABOVE: THE HALF-HEIGHT GLASS WALL OF THIS MEZZANINE ALLOWS SMALLER CHILDREN TO BE SEEN FROM THE ROOM BELOW.

RIGHT: HERE, A SIMPLE PLATFORM CREATES A RELATIVELY PRIVATE DEN UNDER THE EAVES.

The humour transfusion everyone's hanging out for!

B RUGBY
1865

The family kitchen

In many households the kitchen serves as the heart of the home, fulfilling many different functions alongside its primary purpose. It may be a domestic nerve centre as well as an eating area, a place where children play or tackle homework, and somewhere to entertain friends and family. Needless to say, family kitchens work best if they are generous in scale. To gain extra space, you can knock down dividing walls to absorb adjacent rooms or hallways, or extend out into the garden, either to the side or to the rear of your home. An easy connection with outdoor areas, so that children can run in and out under parental supervision, can be a great asset.

- The kitchen is potentially one of the most hazardous areas in the home. Ensure you take proper safety precautions.

- A noticeboard and calendar in a prominent location allows everyone to keep track of domestic admin and key dates.
- You may wish to paint a portion of a wall with blackboard paint to provide a chalk board for children to scribble on.
- When children are very young and play is largely floor-based, it can be a good idea to buy a padded and washable mat to lay over the existing flooring; make sure that you place a non-slip mat underneath it. Incorporating toy storage in the kitchen will prevent needless trips up and down the stairs and helps to keep the floor safely clear of clutter.
- Small children like to help. Involving them in simple kitchen chores such as sweeping the floor or washing up teaches them new skills and increases their self-esteem.

LEFT: A ROBUST, NON-SLIP FLOOR IS ESSENTIAL IN THE KITCHEN. PAY ATTENTION TO SAFETY AS WELL AS AESTHETICS WHEN CHOOSING KITCHEN SURFACES.

FAR LEFT: AN ISLAND UNIT MEANS THAT FOOD PREPARATION CAN TAKE PLACE FACING THE EATING AREA, TURNING THE KITCHEN INTO A SOCIABLE HUB.

The family bathroom

The bathroom is one area of the home where many families feel pressed for space. As with the family kitchen, the larger a family bathroom is the better. A bathroom that is generous in size will allow you to add more fittings – double sinks, for example, or a shower as well as a bath – so that more than one family member can wash and bathe at the same time. An even more practical option is to increase the number of bathrooms or, if that is not possible, to add a separate toilet or cloakroom. A small washbasin and mirror in a teenager's room can also help to ease bottlenecks caused by protracted hair-washing or grooming.

- For small children, bathtime provides the perfect opportunity for water play. It is a good idea to make all bathroom surfaces and finishes fully waterproof.
- Bathrooms can be made accessible to small children with moveable steps or stools, toilet trainer seats and similar accessories. Always use a non-slip mat in the bathtub or shower.
- Good storage is essential. If you keep medicines in the bathroom, make sure the cabinet is lockable.
- A wet room, where the shower drains directly to the floor, makes a practical alternative to a conventional bathroom. The downside of a wet room, however, is that it tends to rule out much in the way of storage.

ABOVE: INSTALLING DOUBLE SINKS IN A FAMILY BATHROOM CAN EASE THE PRESSURE ON TIME AT THE BEGINNING AND END OF THE DAY.

RIGHT: WET ROOMS, SUCH AS THIS GENEROUS SLATE-TILED DOUBLE SHOWER, MAKE GOOD ALTERNATIVES TO STANDARD BATHROOMS, ESPECIALLY WHERE SPACE IS TIGHT. GOOD VENTILATION IS IMPORTANT.

Playrooms & dens

If you have enough space, or an attic or basement ripe for conversion, a separate playroom, family room or den can help to ease the pressure on other areas of the home. In the early years, a playroom can serve as the modern-day equivalent of the Victorian 'day nursery', a separate space that is organized and furnished to suit children's needs, with accessible low storage units and shelves, play tables and the like. Later on, it can morph into a teenage den for playing computer games, chilling out with friends or band practice. In the latter case, you might want to consider adding acoustic insulation to the floor, walls and ceiling, as much

for the sake of your neighbours' peace and quiet as well as your own. A sofa bed or similar arrangement that provides accommodation for the occasional overnight stay is another useful addition, particularly if you would otherwise find yourself in the role of late-night chauffeur.

Playrooms and dens do not have to be relegation zones where children are excluded from the rest of the household. Instead they can provide a place where the whole family can enjoy the type of games and pursuits that would otherwise take up too much space, from playing table tennis and table football to mucking about with train sets and car tracks.

LEFT: THIS PLAYROOM STORAGE IS LOW AND READILY ACCESSIBLE BY SMALL CHILDREN. THE RESILIENT CARPET IS IDEAL FOR FLOOR-BASED GAMES.

ABOVE: A FAMILY ROOM OR DEN IS THE IDEAL PLACE FOR NOISY OR SPACE-HUNGRY PURSUITS SUCH AS PLAYING PINBALL.

Safety & childproofing

The average household presents hundreds of hazards to the health and safety of children, and unfortunately many accidents happen at home. All parents have a responsibility to protect their children from harm and it is important to make sure your home is thoroughly childproofed when you first start a family. At the same time, over-protectiveness does not help children learn independence and how to judge potential risk.

The need for vigilance is undoubtedly greatest in the early years, when children do not yet have full motor control and are programmed to try anything. Later on you can afford to relax your guard a little and place the emphasis on lessons in common sense.

Fire

- Never leave children unattended with a real fire, gas fire or lit candles. Make sure open fires (including gas fires) have protective screens or fireguards.
- Fit a smoke alarm and check it regularly to make sure the batteries are working.
- Make sure all gas fires and appliances are fitted with childproof controls. Have them serviced regularly.
- Fireplaces in regular use should be swept annually and inspected to ensure that the chimney lining is intact, otherwise there is a risk of toxic fumes escaping into upper rooms.
- Socket covers prevent little children from 'exploring' power points.

Water

- When children are small, it is best to do without water features in the garden. Children can drown even in very shallow ponds.
- Never leave a child unsupervised in the bath or in a paddling pool.
- Thermostatic controls on showers allow you to set the water temperature so there is less risk that a child might scold themselves.
- Use a non-slip rubber bathmat in the bathtub or shower.

LEFT: LOOSE RUGS OR RUNNERS SHOULD BE LAID OVER NON-SLIP MATS TO AVOID ACCIDENTAL TUMBLES.

RIGHT: ONLY USE TOYS DESIGNED FOR WATER PLAY IN THE BATHTUB: ANYTHING ELECTRICALLY POWERED OR BREAKABLE COULD PROVE A SERIOUS HAZARD.

Continued

Safety & childproofing

Toxic substances

- Many ordinary household products are toxic if they are ingested and can cause serious harm if splashed on the skin or in the eyes. Check the label if you are unsure whether or not a substance is safe. Keep cleansers, bleach, paint, seals, varnishes, insecticides, pesticides and glue safely under lock and key. Fit childproof locks to household cupboards.
- Keep all medicines in a locked medicine cabinet well out of children's reach.
- Never lock a first-aid box. When you need it, you want to be able to access its contents fast. Store it on a high shelf.

Preventing accidents

- Avoid trailing flexes that may cause children to trip up. Use a cable tidy.

- Keep light fittings and flexes out of the reach of young children. The same goes for the flexes of appliances such as kettles.
- Stair carpets should be fully secured.
- Loose rugs should be laid over non-slip mats.
- Ensure that tall and heavy bookcases are anchored to the wall with brackets.
- Fit window locks to windows on upper levels.
- Restrict bunk beds to children over six years old and ensure ladders are securely anchored.
- Make sure that large expanses of window are fitted with safety glass, which fractures into harmless pebbles if it is broken. Alternatively apply safety film.
- A stair gate is a sensible precaution when a child is learning to walk.
- Corner protectors can be a good idea for sharp table or counter edges.

LEFT: MAKE SURE THAT ART MATERIALS, INCLUDING PAINTS, PLASTICINE, PENS AND CRAYONS ARE NON-TOXIC AND PREFERABLY NON-STAINING.

ABOVE: STOWING EQUIPMENT AWAY IN CHILDPROOFED CUPBOARDS AND KEEPING SURFACES CLEAN AND TIDY REDUCES THE RISK OF ACCIDENTS IN THE KITCHEN.

INTRODUCTION

PLANNING &
DESIGN

FURNITURE &
FITTINGS

DÉCOR & DETAIL

Basic considerations

One of the great challenges when it comes to furnishing and fitting out children's rooms is making the right distinction between items that have an unnecessarily limited appeal and usefulness, and those that will stay the course. A good deal of what is marketed as nursery furniture is designed to tug at the heartstrings of parents-to-be or new mums and dads rather than address the specific needs of a young child.

- In the early years, children need and benefit from furniture and specific items of basic kit that suit their small size and levels of mobility; cots, high chairs and accessible low-level storage are all essentials.
- Avoid miniature chests of drawers and wardrobes, which may have an emotional appeal, but will not remain a practical storage solution for very long. The same is true of furniture that displays a very specific nursery style: you might find that your children will prefer something less 'babyish' a lot sooner than you think.
- Safety is a key consideration. Opt for products from reputable manufacturers and retailers with a trusted brand name to ensure that whatever you buy has been thoroughly tested for safety and performance.
- If you accept hand-me-downs from family or friends, make sure that whatever is being passed on to you is still up to the job it will be required to do.

ABOVE: DECORATIVE BACK-LIT WALL PANELS MAKE AN INTRIGUING DISPLAY FOR CHILDREN OF ANY AGE.

RIGHT: THIS ROBUST CUSTOM-BUILT BUNK BED ARRANGEMENT HAS UNDERBED STORAGE DRAWERS AND SNUG PINE PANELLING.

Beds & sleeping areas

Infants & babies

Sleep is essential for a child's healthy growth and development right from day one as it is in deep, non-dreaming sleep that growth hormones are released. In the early days it is especially important to create the right conditions so that your child can sleep comfortably and safely. Research into SIDS (Sudden Infant Death Syndrome, or 'cot death') has identified a number of key factors to consider and these apply whether your baby's first bed is a Moses basket, carrycot or high-sided cot.

- Until a baby is about six months old, it is advisable to keep the cot in your bedroom so that you can keep a watchful eye on things.
- The recommended sleeping posture for small babies is on their backs.
- Do not use pillows or duvets for babies under a year old to prevent the risk of over-heating (a contributory factor to cot death) or smothering. Similarly, do not let them sleep with large soft toys.
- Cot bedding must suit the size of the cot, not be doubled over or folded down single bed sheets and blankets. Tuck in the sheets and blankets from halfway down the mattress so that the baby can only wriggle upwards, not underneath the covers.
- Position the cot out of draughts and away from sources of heat, such as a radiator.
- Always use a new mattress, ideally for each child. Avoid ventilated mattresses.

ABOVE: POSITION COTS WHERE THEY WILL NOT BE EXPOSED EITHER TO DRAUGHTS OR TO HOT SUNSHINE.

LEFT: MANY COTS COME WITH ADJUSTABLE SIDES; SOME ALLOW THE BASE TO BE LOWERED AS CHILDREN GROW AND ARE ABLE TO PULL THEMSELVES UP TO STANDING.

Continued

Beds & sleeping areas

Young children

By the age of about three or so, your child will be ready to make the transition from a cot to their first proper bed. It is a big step for a young child and can seem unnecessarily momentous if the move coincides with the arrival of a new brother or sister. It is best to try to arrange the timing to prevent your child from feeling usurped.

A full-sized well-made single bed should see your child through to adulthood. There is a wide variety on the market, ranging from those with wooden or metal bedsteads to divan beds. Beds that incorporate storage drawers or a second pull-out bed can be great space savers. A good quality supportive mattress is essential.

Bunk beds

With their compact two-tier arrangement, bunk beds are a space-saving solution where children are sharing a bedroom. Most kids find them appealing, although who gets the coveted top bunk might prove a source of contention. Safety is a key consideration. Children under the age of six should not sleep in the top bunk.

Make sure that the bunk beds are solidly built and conform to safety standards that govern issues such as the size of gaps between slats or framework, the distance between ladder rungs, or the height of guard rails. Mattresses should also fit securely. If possible, it is advisable to view bunk beds fully assembled before buying.

ABOVE: A LOW-LEVEL SINGLE BED IS A GOOD CHOICE FOR THIS ATTIC CONVERSION WHERE HEAD HEIGHT IS LIMITED. WHITE WALLS CREATE AN AIRY FEEL.

RIGHT: THESE CURTAINED, WOOD-PANELLED BUNKS HAVE ALL THE COSY APPEAL OF SLEEPER COMPARTMENTS IN AN OVERNIGHT FERRY.

Continued

Beds & sleeping areas

Older children

If you invested in a bed of decent quality when your child was small, it should last right through the teenage years and beyond. The same will probably not be true of the mattress. During the growth spurts of adolescence, your child will need a mattress that gives proper support.

Of all items of furniture, beds see the most use and it is the mattress that chiefly takes the punishment. By the time children become teenagers, a mattress might have seen a fair degree of wear and tear. To a small child, a mattress is a handy springboard to action, no matter how often they are told not to treat their bed as a trampoline. Lumpy or sagging mattresses, or those with rips and tears in the cover, need to be replaced.

Where space is tight, as it might be if your teenager has moved out of a shared room into a smaller room of their own, a variation on the bunk bed idea can be a good solution. Many companies produce modular systems that combine a high-level sleeping platform with a study area beneath. This kind of arrangement can also be custom-built to your own specification. Robust construction is essential.

LEFT: COMPACT AND PRACTICAL: A SOFA BED FOR OVERNIGHT VISITORS AND A WORKING AREA ARE SLOTTED IN UNDERNEATH A HIGH-LEVEL BED.

FAR LEFT: A DIVAN BED UPHOLSTERED IN PURPLE, A FUNKY MODERN CHAIR AND A DEEP-PILE RUG UPDATE THIS TEENAGE BEDROOM.

Seating

When it comes to chairs and other forms of seating, one size will not fit all. From baby bouncers and car seats to high chairs and bean bags, there is a wide variety of seating specially designed for children at different stages of development. It is important to research the market thoroughly and think carefully about performance and function, particularly in the case of products marketed for babies and toddlers. Aspects to consider include: comfort, robustness and rigidity, weight, stability, portability, whether the seat or chair can be folded or washed, and ease of use. Many of these seats and chairs will only be required for a limited period of time and hand-me-down or second-hand outlets can be acceptable sources provided the item is in good condition to start with.

ABOVE: SQUASHY BEAN BAGS OR LARGE FLOOR CUSHIONS ARE IDEAL FOR LOUNGING TEENAGERS. INFLATABLE CHAIRS ALSO MAKE FUN SEATS.

RIGHT: THE WINDOW SEAT, PART OF THE ROOM AND YET SET ASIDE FROM IT, IS ETERNALLY APPEALING FOR CHILDREN AND ADULTS ALIKE.

Continued

Seating

- **Rockers & nursing chairs** Babies are soothed by movement and a rocking chair may be an asset in the early days. Specially designed low, armless nursing chairs allow you to sit in a comfortable posture for feeding with your feet flat on the floor.
- **Baby bouncers** The baby bouncer is a useful piece of kit for the early weeks and months. The seat supports the baby securely while permitting gentle bouncing or rocking movements at a stage when a child cannot yet sit unsupported. Never leave a baby unattended in a bouncer or baby seat.

- **Car seats** The safest and easiest to use car seats tend to be the most expensive, but this is not an area where you should economize. Car seats come in forward- and rear-facing models and in different sizes to suit different ages and weights.
- **High chairs** There is a huge range of high chairs on the market: restaurant-style chairs that allow you to pull the child up to the table, chairs with integral trays that fold away when not in use, and chairs with adjustable seat and foot plates that 'grow' with your child. High chairs get regularly splattered, so look out for finishes that are easy to wipe down.
- **Booster seats** A booster seat allows a child who has outgrown a high chair to sit at the right level at the table.
- **Play chairs** Instead of raising a child up to your level, play chairs, like the mini chairs you see in nurseries or crèches, allow younger children to sit at a height that is comfortable for them. Many play chairs come in sets with tables that can be used for creative pursuits, games or having snacks. Alternatively, stacking stools can serve the same purpose.
- **Floor cushions & bean bags** For older children, floor cushions make great impromptu seats when hanging out with friends. Bean bags are another good place to slump.

LEFT: THE BUBBLE CHAIR BY SCANDINAVIAN DESIGNER EERO AARNIO IS A 1960S CLASSIC THAT IS IRRESISTIBLE TO CHILDREN OF ALL AGES.

FAR LEFT: MINI PLAY FURNITURE ALLOWS CHILDREN TO SIT AT A HEIGHT THAT IS COMFORTABLE FOR THEM.

Play areas

Play is how children explore the world and an important means of learning in the pre-school years. Designing and equipping successful play areas for children means first of all looking at the world through their eyes. All too often adults do the imagining on behalf of the children, which leads to trophy purchases such as the hand-carved rocking horse that no one ever sits on, the heirloom doll's house that has 'don't touch' written all over it, or the latest must-have toy that provides amusement for the best part of an hour before the novelty wears off.

A better guide for inspiration is the way a good nursery is laid out and equipped. There will be areas for wet play, plenty of scrap materials for creative activities, space for running around in the fresh air and letting off steam, and quiet story corners. At home, the wet area might well be the kitchen, where spills can be mopped up, and likewise the kitchen table is a good place for colouring and sticking; the letting off steam area might be the back garden or the local park; and the quiet story corner might be your child's bedside, but the basic idea is the same.

ABOVE: CHILDREN LIKE THEIR TOYS AND GAMES TO BE OUT ON VIEW AND READILY ACCESSIBLE, PARTICULARLY IN THE EARLY YEARS. BREAKABLE THINGS CAN BE STORED AWAY FOR LATER.

RIGHT: WHAT COULD PROVIDE A BETTER SPRINGBOARD FOR THE IMAGINATION THAN A TREEHOUSE?

Continued

Play areas

Points to consider

- Mucking about with paints, crayons and magic markers can be a messy business, so it is best to confine these activities to areas that are easy to clean up.

- When children are small, any surface is a potential place for mark-making. Restrict access to art materials to times when you can be there to supervise.

- Hand-in-hand with creative play goes display. Pin up your child's latest efforts on a noticeboard in the kitchen or their bedroom so they can feel proud of their work.

- Rye grass or hard-wearing utility grass seed will withstand greater punishment if your children like to use the lawn as a sports pitch.

- Sandpits or sandboxes should be covered when not in use to keep them dry and prevent fouling by animals.

- Outdoor play equipment is good for letting off steam and learning coordination and motor skills. Make sure equipment has been designed and constructed to safety standards. Anchor it securely and provide safe surfacing, such as bark chippings, underneath.

- Play inevitably means toys, but it does not necessarily mean sharing your entire home with brightly coloured plastic. Improvised toys and games can be just as satisfying and stimulating – from the pots and pans that absorb a toddler to the bedspread draped over chairs that makes a secret den for a five-year-old.

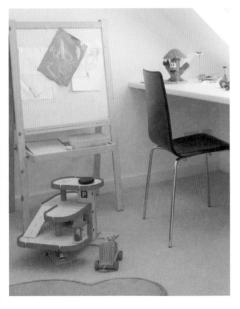

LEFT: A CHILD-SIZED EASEL MAKES AN IDEAL SURFACE FOR PAINTING AND DRAWING, ALONG WITH A PLACE TO STORE ART MATERIALS.

FAR LEFT: THIS LARGE-SCALE WORLD MAP WITH MAGNETIC LABELS IS INTERACTIVE, EDUCATIONAL AND VISUALLY STIMULATING.

Study areas

Soon after your child starts school, you will need to think about how to provide the right conditions for study, which is as much about encouraging the right approach and attitude as it is about fixtures and fittings. Early on, many children prefer to tackle their homework on the kitchen table where help is at hand. Most parents prefer it that way, too, if only to ensure that the work actually gets done. But bustling family kitchens do not generally offer the peace and quiet required for more extensive bouts of concentration. Once homework is set on a regular basis, and when tests and exams loom, your child will need a dedicated area to work.

Ideally, each child should have a study area in their bedroom. If space is very tight and that is not possible, then you may be able to set aside part of a living room for the purpose. You can screen a study area in a multipurpose space by partitioning it in some way with a screen or divider to signal the shift of activity. Alternatively, you can house a study or work station within a wall of fitted cupboards so that it can be concealed from view when not in use.

ABOVE: A TRADITIONAL-STYLE KNEEHOLE DESK WITH A MATCHING CHAIR WORKS WELL IN A GIRL'S BEDROOM.

RIGHT: IF SPACE IS TIGHT, A LONG NARROW WORK SURFACE MAKES A PRACTICAL SOLUTION. GOOD NATURAL LIGHT IS IMPORTANT FOR WORKING AREAS.

Continued

Study areas

Points to consider

- Anyone sitting for relatively long periods working on a computer or writing needs a supportive desk chair, and this is true of children as much as it is of adults. You do not have to break the bank buying an ergonomic task chair for your child, but it is advisable to invest in one that provides proper support and which is adjustable to some degree.

- As with nursery furniture generally, desks specifically designed for children will be outgrown relatively quickly. What is required instead is a sufficiently large surface for a child or teenager to spread out books and papers and access a computer. Work tables designed

for home offices can be a practical choice, as can folding trestles. Some modular systems incorporate a desk area with integral storage.

- Focused task lighting aids concentration. An anglepoise or similar adjustable desk light can be targeted to provide a boost of illumination on the page or keyboard. Uplighting is recommended as background lighting for work that involves staring at a computer screen.

- Some children are naturally more organized than others. A noticeboard provides a useful place for pinning up schedules and other important pieces of paper than might otherwise go astray at the bottom of a rucksack or schoolbag.

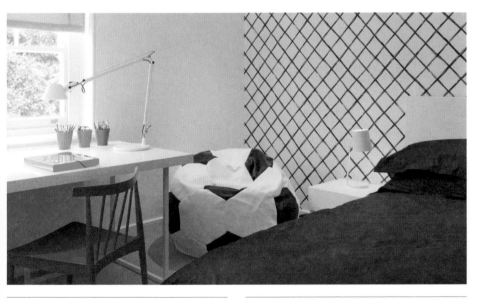

LEFT: WHERE THE DESK IS A BUILT-IN WORKTOP, YOU WILL NEED TO PROVIDE ADDITIONAL STORAGE FOR PAPERWORK, SUCH AS THIS SMALL METAL UNIT.

ABOVE: AN ADJUSTABLE TASK LIGHT WILL BOOST AMBIENT LIGHT WHEN NECESSARY. ALL STUDY AREAS SHOULD BE PROPERLY LIT.

Storage

Planning

Keeping on top of belongings is one of the great challenges of family life. The arrival of children brings with it whole new categories of possessions and equipment, from toys and games, to sports kit and treasured pieces of artwork – great quantities of objects that grow exponentially with each birthday and Christmas. If you do not plan ahead, you will run out of places to put things within a relatively short period of time.

In the family home, storage cannot be approached in a reactive fashion. When a child's toys no longer fit in a single basket, box or container, the answer is not necessarily to buy another one. From the outset, it is important to incorporate as much storage as possible both within a child's room and in other areas around the home. This may mean using between-spaces – such as halls, corridors and landings – as dedicated storage areas that are fitted out with shelving or cupboards, or it may mean using attics, basements and garages for items that are required infrequently or on a seasonal basis.

The other side of the equation is taking every opportunity to review possessions and get rid of what is out-grown, either in a physical or developmental sense. This calls for an element of diplomacy because most children will have favourite toys they want to hang onto.

LEFT: THESE MODULAR CUBBYHOLES MAKE GREAT STOWING PLACES FOR TOYS AND CLOTHING ALIKE.

RIGHT: FITTED CUPBOARDS EXPLOIT THE FULL HEIGHT OF A BABY'S ROOM AND WILL ACCOMMODATE GROWING NUMBERS OF POSSESSIONS AS THE CHILD GETS OLDER.

Continued

Storage

Types of storage

When it comes to storage, the fundamental choice is between fitted and unfitted, or built-in and freestanding. Whichever system you choose should have as much to do with basic practicality as it does with stylistic preference.

- Fitted storage, such as cupboards, closets and shelving, plays an important role in the family home as a means of organizing everyday clutter as unobtrusively as possible, especially where storage is incorporated into shared areas such as living rooms, or slotted into hallways and other between-spaces. Concealed or fitted storage is ideal for storing bulky items such as buggies or outdoor clothing and gear.
- Unfitted storage, such as chests of drawers and containers of various descriptions, can prove to be the most flexible and practical option in children's rooms. This is especially true in the early years, when children like to see their belongings around them and need to be able to access them as easily as possible. Containers are ideal for collections of toys and games, and help keep vital pieces together.
- Built-in or modular solutions can help your teenager to keep their clutter under control.
- Avoid the temptation to buy miniaturized items of storage furniture, particularly those decorated with nursery motifs. Children's belongings accumulate so quickly that such pieces will be outgrown in the blink of an eye, both in terms of capacity and visual appeal.

ABOVE: HERE, FITTED STORAGE MEANS HOUSEHOLD CLUTTER IS CONCEALED BEHIND NEAT WHITE PANELS.

LEFT: POCKETED FABRIC TIDIES ARE PERFECT FOR ORGANIZING SHOES AND BASIC ITEMS OF KIT.

Continued

Storage

Clothes

- Despite the fact that few babies have large wardrobes, a decent-sized chest of drawers is a good investment right at the outset. In the early months it can be used to store nappies, bedding and baby products as well as clothes; if the top is a convenient height, it can also double up as a changing surface.

- Low-level shelving, rails and hooks that can be reached by small children help encourage them to dress themselves.

- Where two children are sharing a room, make sure that they each have their own clothes storage to avoid disputes.

- The requirement for hanging space increases as a child grows older. Options include fitting out an alcove with a clothes rail, buying a freestanding clothes rail of the type used in retail environments, or buying a freestanding wardrobe of some description. High or heavy items of furniture should always be securely bracketed to the wall.

- Because children grow so fast, it is important to keep ahead of the game and instigate periodic reviews so that you can get rid of or recycle any item of clothing that is outgrown or worn out.

- Large storage drawers incorporated into the base of beds are good places for bulky jumpers, blankets or spare bedding.

ABOVE: HERE, AN ENTIRE WALL IS GIVEN OVER TO BUILT-IN STORAGE. WHEN STORAGE IS AS SEAMLESS AS THIS, YOU MAY NEED A DIAGRAM TO REMIND YOU WHERE EVERYTHING IS KEPT.

RIGHT: HANGING CLOTHES AT A LOW LEVEL KEEPS THEM EASILY ACCESSIBLE AND ON VIEW.

Continued

Storage

Toys & games

In the early months and years, your children will be playing under your watchful eye. That means you may need storage provision for toys and games not simply in your child's room, but also in the kitchen and living area too.

Containers that are relatively light, rigid and portable are indispensable for toy storage. In the first year, one or two of these will probably be adequate. Later on, you can add more to keep up with your child's possessions, sorting toys by type, or by ownership. It is better to have multiple containers of a manageable size, particularly those that can be stacked, rather than a few very large containers that invite children to tip the entire contents onto the floor. Small containers, such as storage jars, are also invaluable for organizing everything from art supplies to Lego.

Many toys and games are easy to shelve. In the early years, make sure that shelving, whether built-in or freestanding, is set at a low level to avoid the risk of children mountaineering to reach a toy on a high shelf. A magazine rack can be very versatile: books can be kept with their covers facing forwards, making it easier for children to make their selection based on the picture on the front.

LEFT: UNDERBED STORAGE CAN BE USED TO HOUSE TOYS AND GAMES IN THE EARLY YEARS.

FAR LEFT: CHILDREN'S BOOKS ARE STORED ON THE LOWER SHELVES OF THIS FAMILY BOOKCASE.

Continued

Storage

Hobbies, kit & homework

As children grow and develop new interests, good organization becomes more important than providing a reassuring display of favourite toys within arm's reach. While many teenagers regard the floor as the only storage space worth bothering about, their storage needs are no less acute than any other family member.

- Bulky items, such as sports equipment, should ideally be stored away from the children's room, preferably in fitted storage where it can be conveniently retrieved. You may wish to rotate sports kit used on a seasonal basis in and out of deep storage areas in attics, basements or garages.
- Encourage children to keep their musical instruments in their cases when they are not being played to prevent damage.
- A desk with drawers, or a separate narrow filing cabinet, is a useful way for a teenager to organize paperwork, files, and so on. Box files that can be stored on open shelving are another solution.
- Plenty of shelving will be required for books, magazines, CDs and DVDs.
- A noticeboard near the desk is a good way of keeping track of schedules, lists and other important bits of paper.
- Racks and rails can be used to keep the floor area as clear as possible.

ABOVE: ENCOURAGE OLDER CHILDREN TO BACK UP THEIR DIGITAL AND MUSIC FILES REGULARLY TO PRESERVE IMPORTANT DATA.

RIGHT: MODULAR SHELVING SYSTEMS OFTEN INCLUDE DRAWER UNITS. WALL-MOUNTED SUPPORTS ALLOW YOU TO DETERMINE THE SPACING TO YOUR OWN SATISFACTION.

INTRODUCTION
PLANNING & DESIGN
FURNITURE & FITTINGS
DÉCOR & DETAIL

Basic considerations

Decorating children's rooms means addressing practical issues first and foremost. But it does not mean that you have to adopt a strictly utilitarian approach. It is perfectly possible to come up with a scheme that is both easy on the eye and easy to live with. The same is true elsewhere in the family home.

■ When children are small, it is best to accept the fact that accidents will happen. This means choosing surfaces and finishes that are robust and hard-wearing, and avoiding any finish or material that might be irredeemably damaged by the rough and tumble of daily life.

■ Many natural materials can take a fair degree of punishment and still look good, with wear and tear contributing to their character.

■ Stylish expanses of glass and stainless steel will show every smudge and mark, and require a lot of time and effort to keep clean.

■ Choosing washable loose covers for upholstered furniture, or flooring that can be mopped clean after a spill, means that you will not have to be on constant alert.

■ Another key aspect to consider is comfort. Softer, more resilient surfaces underfoot are more comfortable for children to play on, and less rackety and noisy.

RIGHT: IN THIS NURSERY, BRIGHT COLOUR IS DELIVERED TO A NEUTRAL DÉCOR THROUGH THE SOFT FURNISHINGS AND SCREEN. THESE CAN BE EASILY CHANGED TO SUIT MORE GROWN-UP TASTES LATER ON.

LEFT: PAINT IS QUICK AND EASY TO CHANGE, IF YOUR LITTLE GIRL HAS HER HEART SET ON A DECORATIVE SCHEME FIT FOR A FAIRY PRINCESS.

Décor schemes

Many parents view the decoration of children's rooms as an opportunity to release their own inner child. There is nothing wrong with this approach as long as you know what you are letting yourself in for. A themed nursery, with coordinating wallpaper, curtains, borders and friezes may be cute and appealing but it will not be appropriate for long. Unless you are prepared to redecorate often, it is usually best to keep the basic surfaces and finishes relatively plain, and ring the changes with soft furnishings and other details that are easy and economic to replace.

Colour

From very early on, babies are stimulated by colour and studies have shown that the first colour they recognize is orangey red. While walls painted in strong, vivid shades might be a little overwhelming for small children, accents of bright colour are always playful and uplifting. By the time your children approach the teenage years, it is fair to allow them to express their own tastes in colour.

When choosing background colours for walls or flooring, pay attention to the quality of natural light. Choose colours from the warm end of the spectrum, such as tones of yellow, orange or red, for rooms that have a northern orientation (southern in the Southern Hemisphere). Rooms that face south can take cooler colours such as blue and blue-grey.

ABOVE: DREAMS OF FLYING ARE GUARANTEED IN THIS AERONAUTICAL BEDROOM. A VIVID COLOUR SCHEME OF RED, WHITE AND BLUE HAS GREAT GRAPHIC IMPACT.

RIGHT: A VIVID ALPHABET PAPER FORMS AN EYE-CATCHING FEATURE WALL IN A YOUNG CHILD'S BEDROOM.

Continued

Décor schemes

Pattern

Whether they are stylized, figurative or abstract, all patterns have an inherent sense of rhythm and movement due to the repetitive nature of the design. Small babies are intrigued by strong shapes and graphic contrast, and a room that was entirely plain and neutral would not provide the visual stimulation they need. However, it is important not to overdo it.

There are many patterns designed specifically for children on the market, in applications ranging from wallpaper and rugs, to duvet covers, curtain and upholstery fabric. As with themed decoration in general, many of these will only appeal for a limited amount of time, so it is best to opt for generic or classic designs, such as checks and stripes, for large surface areas. Restrict more specific or figurative patterns to elements that are easy to change.

Texture

In the context of children's rooms, texture is all about comfort. Children are often very sensitive to how things feel simply because they have more physical contact with surfaces such as flooring, for example. Smooth or soft surfaces are kinder to young skin than scratchy or more abrasive ones, which tends to rule out some types of natural fibre flooring. Embossed or textured wall coverings also tend to pick up dirt more readily, so it is a better idea to opt for smooth, washable finishes.

LEFT: THE TEXTURAL VARIETY PROVIDED BY THE QUILTED BEDCOVER AND FLUFFY RUG ADD INTEREST TO THIS SUBTLE AND RESTFUL COLOUR SCHEME.

ABOVE: SIMPLE GEOMETRIC WALLPAPER PATTERNS HAVE A LONGER LIFESPAN THAN THOSE THAT ARE SPECIALLY THEMED FOR CHILDREN.

Window treatments

Relatively affordable and easy to change, window treatments in children's rooms can be used to display patterns and motifs that have a short-lived appeal. Otherwise, in rooms that are already visually busy, you may wish to restrict your choice to plain or textured designs, or those with a simple geometric pattern.

Practical considerations

- Whichever type of window treatment you choose, make sure that it can be fully raised or drawn back clear of the glass to admit the maximum amount of natural light during the day. Children's rooms that are half-shrouded in gloom are not pleasant or safe places to play.

- When children are small, curtains or blinds should not extend below sill level, so that they will not present a climbing temptation.

- Make sure that all window treatments are securely fixed or suspended from robust track or rods, otherwise a sharp tug might send them crashing down.

- Fit window locks, sash stoppers or similar restrictors to windows on upper stories.

- If your child finds it hard to sleep when it is still light outside, you can line curtains with blackout material or use blackout blinds. Interlined curtains also muffle sound and provide more insulation.

- Ensure that the window treatment is easy to maintain, which means using washable fabrics for curtains or wipe-clean blinds.

ABOVE: FOLDING WOODEN SHUTTERS WITH ADJUSTABLE LOUVRES ALLOW FINE LIGHT CONTROL AND ARE EASY TO DUST AND MAINTAIN.

RIGHT: THIS ROMAN BLIND IN A STRIPED FABRIC MAKES A NEAT AND TAILORED WINDOW TREATMENT THAT WILL NOT DATE TOO QUICKLY.

Continued

Window treatments

Curtains

With a softer appearance than blinds, curtains are every bit as effective at screening light provided they are made from a substantial fabric and fully lined. Tailored or pleated headings are a little formal for children's rooms. Instead, opt for simple tape headings, gathered headings, or cased headings (where the rod is slotted through a channel of fabric at the top of the curtain). Alternatively you can buy curtains with tab tops that are suspended from a rod or rail.

Blinds

Blinds come in a wide range of materials and styles and make a practical, no-nonsense window treatment for children's rooms. Most economic are simple cotton roller blinds that can be tailored to suit different window sizes. Roman blinds, which draw up into neat horizontal pleats, are another fabric option. Slatted Venetian blinds or vertical louvres, made in wood or coated aluminium, offer a greater degree of light control and enable you to filter strong sun on hot days.

Drapery

In the early years, trailing drapery is impractical in children's rooms and may even present a hazard. Older girls, however, often like the type of pretty, impromptu effects you can achieve by looping a length of filmy fabric over a pole or rod. You can combine this type of treatment with a simple roller blind for light control.

ABOVE: HERE, A FLORAL PATTERED BLIND IS COMBINED WITH TRANSPARENT SILL-LENGTH CURTAINS FOR A SOFT AND PRETTY LOOK.

LEFT: IN THIS WHITE PANELLED BEDROOM, THE RED AND WHITE FABRIC CHOSEN FOR THE CURTAINS AND CUSHION COVER LOOKS BRIGHT AND AIRY.

Walls

Walls represent the largest surface area in any room, which means that how you choose to decorate them will have a considerable impact. Children's rooms tend to be visually busy, with plenty on display and much of it brightly coloured, which can be an argument for keeping the walls relatively plain. However you choose to decorate the walls, good preparation is essential.

Preparation
- Clear the room as far as possible and cover everything that remains with drop-sheets.
- Brush down or vacuum the walls to remove loose surface dirt and cobwebs.
- Wash the walls with a non-abrasive, non-foaming cleanser.
- Fill cracks and holes with a proprietary filler. Allow to dry, sand down and fill again until the surface is level.
- If the walls are really battered, or large areas of plasterwork are crumbling and loose, they need replastering.
- An alternative to replastering is cross-lining with lining paper, papering horizontally and then vertically.
- If skirting boards and other types of moulding are clogged with previous coats of paint, you may need to strip these off using a chemical stripper or blowtorch. Fill any holes with woodfiller and sand once dry.
- Prepare walls for painting by applying one or more thinned layers of undercoat.

ABOVE AND RIGHT: TWO APPROACHES TO COLLAGE: A JOINT HOUSEHOLD EFFORT AT DECORATING THE WALL BESIDE THE STAIRS, AND A TEENAGER'S EXPRESSION OF PERSONAL STYLE.

Continued

Walls

Paint

A quick, cheap and easy cover-up for walls, ceilings and woodwork, paint comes in every conceivable colour and in a range of finishes from soft and matt, through to high gloss. If you feel daunted by the choice, many manufacturers produce themed or edited palettes, which can be a good way of narrowing the field down a bit.

- Emulsion or water-based paints are not as durable as eggshell and gloss, which are oil-based and easier to wipe clean.
- The precise tone of a particular shade can be difficult to judge. Some colours that look pale on a colour chart 'mount up', or become more intense when applied to a larger area. Before you make your final selection buy a small

sample pot in your chosen shade and paint a small patch of wall to gauge the effect.

- Always follow manufacturer's instructions when it comes to priming and undercoating your walls.
- Make sure that you buy the right quantity of paint. Many paint manufacturers' websites provide a paint calculator.
- Choose paints that are low in VOCs (volatile organic compounds), which have been shown to cause allergies, skin irritations and asthma. Better still, choose eco paint, which now comes in a much broader range of colours and finishes than before and is just as easy to apply as standard paint.
- Make sure that you air children's rooms thoroughly after decorating.

LEFT: IN THIS LIVING ROOM, A FAVOURITE FAMILY PICTURE BLOWN UP TO WALL-SIZE MAKES A GRAPHIC COUNTERPOINT TO THE CLEAN WHITE DÉCOR.

FAR LEFT: YOU DO NOT HAVE TO PAINT THE ENTIRE ROOM THE SAME COLOUR. PICKING OUT A SINGLE WALL WITH A STRONG COLOUR CAN HAVE GREAT IMPACT.

Continued

Walls

Paper

Wallpaper has long been a favourite wall covering in children's rooms, particularly those designs that feature classic children's themes. If you do not mind redecorating sooner rather than later, wallpaper can be a good way of giving a child's room an instant look.

- Before you commit to a final choice of wallpaper, it is a good idea to pin a sample to the wall so you can assess what the final effect will look like.
- Many wallpapers designed specifically for children come with matching borders and friezes. Alternatively, you can opt for a fresh, graphic pattern such as checks, spots, stripes or simple flowers.

- Some manufacturers produce wallpapers where the paste is applied directly to the wall, which means that all that you have to do is position the drops of paper correctly. This is much easier than applying paste to paper first. Even so, papering requires more skill and patience than painting.
- Vinyl-coated paper allows you to wipe off any smudges or scribbles.

Panelling

Tongue-and-groove panelling applied to a wall or to the lower portions of the wall makes a robust surface that both withstands knocks and scrapes and has a cosy, intimate quality. You can either stain the panelling to seal it or paint it the same colour as the rest of the decoration.

ABOVE: CHOOSING A WALLPAPER FEATURING JUST TWO COLOURS MAKES IT EASY TO COMBINE WITH SOFT FURNISHINGS IN A COMPLEMENTARY COLOUR.

RIGHT: YOU CAN PASTE ALMOST ANYTHING TO THE WALL, PROVIDED THE PAPER IS ROBUST ENOUGH. SEA CHARTS AND MAPS MAKE INTRIGUING BACKDROPS.

Flooring

Our contact with the floor is much more direct than it is with any other surface in the interior. For example, we tend not to go around touching the walls, whereas we may sit, lie or lounge on the floor as well as walk on it. This is even more the case for children, whose play, certainly in the early years, is largely floor-based. Your choice of flooring needs to be made with both comfort and practicality firmly in mind.

Practical considerations

■ How comfortable a floor is – or how much 'give' it has – is largely due to how resilient it is. Cushioned vinyl, linoleum and wood, along with soft flooring such as carpet, are the most comfortable floor surfaces for children, and when they take a tumble, they are less likely to hurt themselves.

■ Think about durability when it comes to choosing flooring. Adult bedrooms see lighter traffic than other areas in the home, which means that flooring can be less durable; in children's rooms, though, the floor generally takes more punishment and will require something more hard wearing.

■ Maintenance is another key factor to consider. How easy is the flooring to keep clean? Does it stain? Are there any treatments or seals that can improve stain-resistance?

■ Smooth or glossy floors, or those that require polishing, may look beautiful, but in a family home they will increase the risk of accidents.

■ Most types of flooring require professional installation.

ABOVE: SCATTER RUGS ARE A GOOD WAY OF ADDING WARMTH, COMFORT AND STYLE UNDERFOOT.

LEFT: RAINBOW STAIRS MAKE A COLOURFUL FEATURE. TO PAINT AREAS OF FLOORING THAT SEE A LOT OF TRAFFIC, USE HARD-WEARING FLOOR OR YACHT PAINT.

Continued

Flooring

Materials

- **Carpet** Warm, resilient and quiet, carpet has much to recommend it as flooring for children's rooms, provided you choose the right type. Avoid deep or velvet pile and opt instead for harder-wearing corded carpet. A small percentage of artificial fibre, such as nylon, blended with wool, increases durability. The risk with carpet is staining: spills should be tackled immediately.

- **Natural-fibre floor coverings** Of all the natural-fibre floorings, seagrass is perhaps the only one suitable for children's rooms, as it is smooth and resistant to spills and stains.

- **Linoleum** Durable, warm, quiet, anti-bacterial and resistant to grease, lino makes a practical and attractive choice for children's rooms, particularly in homes where there are allergy sufferers. It is available in sheet or tile form and in a range of patterns and colours.

- **Cork** Affordable, warm, comfortable and quiet underfoot, cork tiles are also hypo-allergenic and antibacterial. They must be sealed, though, which does increase slipperiness.

- **Vinyl** There is an endless variety of vinyl flooring, ranging widely in price and durability. Many types are patterned to simulate natural materials such as wood or stone.

- **Wood** When it comes to wood flooring, you can either sand existing floorboards, or lay solid wood, manufactured wood or laminate flooring. Some synthetic products are virtually indestructible; real wood, however, will show wear and tear, and requires proper sealing and maintenance. Wood will amplify noise levels unless it is laid over sound-proofing.

ABOVE: SANDED AND REFINISHED FLOORBOARDS MAKE PRACTICAL AND AFFORDABLE FLOORING FOR A FAMILY HOME. RUGS CAN BE USED FOR PLAY AREAS.

RIGHT: CARPET IS WARM, QUIET AND KIND TO YOUNG KNEES. A PATTERNED OR MARLED CARPET WILL SHOW FEWER STAINS SHOULD SPILLS OCCUR.

Lighting

Lighting is no less important in children's rooms than it is elsewhere in the home. You should aim to have good background or ambient light, as well as more focused, brighter light for study areas. While in adult bedrooms and living areas the focus falls on creating a sympathetic atmosphere conducive to relaxation, children's rooms need more illumination. Lighting must be bright enough to allow them to play safely, without being so bright that it creates glare, which is tiring and makes people – even little people – feel out of sorts and ill at ease.

- Make the most of natural light by ensuring that curtains and blinds can be pulled right back or raised well clear of the window.
- Avoid glare. Glare occurs when there is too great a contrast between a light source and its surroundings. Shade bulbs so that light does not shine directly into the eyes, and do not rely solely on a single overhead fixture to light the entire room. On its own, overhead light casts shadows into the corners of the room and has a deadening effect.
- When children are small, avoid table and floor-standing lamps that could be easily tugged over. Similarly, watch out for trailing flexes.

ABOVE: ADJUSTABLE LIGHT FITTINGS CAN BE USED TO TARGET SPECIFIC AREAS, WHICH IS IDEAL FOR ACTIVITIES SUCH AS READING OR WRITING DIARIES.

LEFT: A SPECIALLY COMMISSIONED NEON ARTWORK LITERALLY PUTS A CHILD'S NAME UP IN LIGHTS AND EMITS A SOOTHING GLOW AT BEDTIME.

Continued

Lighting

- **Pendants & other central fixtures** Overhead lights can make a striking central feature, but they should not be used as the sole light source in a room.
- **Wall lights** Wall-mounted fittings provide a good level of background light without the risk of glare.
- **Tracklights & spotlights** Ceiling-mounted tracklights or spotlights are another a good means of supplying background light without glare. Individual spots can be angled to reflect light from the planes of walls or the ceiling.
- **Uplighting** Fixed or freestanding uplights bounce light off the ceiling and provide soft background illumination.

- **Task lights** Older children will require a task light to boost illumination in a study area. Close concentrated work requires higher light levels than relaxing. An adjustable task light is the most versatile option and can double-up as a bedside lamp.
- **Nightlights** These plug directly into a socket to provide a reassuring glow for children who are either scared of the dark or need to get up after bedtime to visit the bathroom.
- **Novelty lights** Older children and teenagers often enjoy fun lights such as light-up globes, lava lamps, glow balls and fibre-optic lights.
- **Bedside light** This should be bright enough for story time or reading in bed.

LEFT: THIS TRADITIONAL SHADED BEDSIDE LIGHT CREATES A WARM AND WELCOMING AMBIENCE.

RIGHT: DECORATIVE LIGHTS ARE PLAYFUL AND UPLIFTING. THIS PRETTY BRANCHED DESIGN IS FITTED WITH LONG-LASTING LOW-VOLTAGE LIGHTS.

Soft furnishings

From blankets and cushions to rugs and curtains, soft furnishings are all about comfort in its widest sense – rooms with uniformly hard surfaces and finishes simply do not have the same appeal as those furnished with textiles. However, many fabrics will mark and stain easily. In children's rooms, as well as the family home in general, you need to ensure that all soft furnishings are durable and preferably washable. Choose robust cotton, cotton canvas and linen union over more delicate materials that will not stand up to wear and tear. Proprietary sprays can offer extra protection to upholstery.

Bedding

- Choose bedding made out of natural fibres wherever possible. Cotton is a naturally absorbent material, which is why it feels so comfortable next to the skin.
- Duvets should not be used for babies under a year old to prevent the risk of over-heating and suffocation.
- Natural sheepskins are widely recommended as bedding for babies. They are springy and resilient, which means they are very comfortable, and the wool fibres help to regulate temperature by trapping warm air when it is cold and by absorbing moisture and keeping the baby cool and dry when it is hot.
- Bedding is a great way of adding personality to a child's room, whether it takes the form of sheets and duvet covers patterned with a favourite cartoon character, a quilt you have made yourself from scraps of fabric, or a colourful blanket.

LEFT: GAUZY MUSLIN DRAPERY SUSPENDED FROM THE CEILING IS AN ECONOMICAL WAY OF CREATING A ROMANTIC CANOPY BED.

FAR LEFT: THIS INDOOR TEEPEE GOES A STEP BEYOND THE IMPROMPTU TENT CREATED BY THROWING A BLANKET OVER A PAIR OF CHAIRS.

Continued

Soft furnishings

Rugs

- Rugs can be laid over all types of flooring to provide additional comfort and interest underfoot. On hard or smooth floors, you must lay them over non-slip matting to prevent accidental tumbles.
- Flat-weave rugs of various descriptions are ideal for children's rooms. Cotton dhurries, Mexican serapes and striped Scandinavian-style runners come in a wide range of vivid colours and designs. Many of these rugs are not colour-fast or shrink-proof, but they can often be machine-washed on a low setting.
- Low pile rugs designed specially for children and shaped or patterned with sports themes or cartoon characters are another popular option for younger children's rooms.

Cushions

- Cushion covers are one of those finishing touches that are economical and easy to change, which means that when your children have outgrown nursery patterns, you can make or buy new covers that reflect their changing tastes.
- Floor cushions and bean bags make great all-purpose seating for small children and teens alike. Choose designs with removable and washable covers. Some large cushions can be zipped together for floor-level reclining.

Special effects

- For the princess in your family, you can drape a length of filmy or sparkly fabric above the bed to create a romantic bower.
- Canopies and tents designed for children's beds create a range of effects, from secret dens to starry skies and rainbows. These are widely available and mostly inexpensive.

ABOVE AND RIGHT: FABRIC THAT FEATURES THEMES SPECIFICALLY DESIGNED FOR CHILDREN ADDS A FUN ELEMENT TO A BEDROOM AND CAN BE CHANGED AT A LATER DATE WITHOUT GREAT EXPENSE.

Display

In many ways, children's rooms are all about display. From toddler-hood through to school-age, younger children like the reassurance of seeing their favourite toys around them, and the same is true of precious pieces of artwork. For the older child and teenager, display becomes all about making statements of identity and allegiance. At any age, what counts is what your child wants on view – you should give them confidence in their choices and preferences, not impose your own taste on them.

- Whatever you put on display should be relatively accessible to your child so that they can retrieve the item when they want to without coming to harm.
- When children are small, hang pictures or put up artwork low down on the wall where they can see them.
- Show children how much you respect their creative work by picking out a few good efforts and having them properly framed.
- Hanging displays can be very eye-catching, whether they are colourful mobiles created by your child, glitter balls, or airfix models suspended from the ceiling.
- The collecting bug often begins in childhood. Group treasures on the top of a chest of drawers or arrange them on shelves for maximum impact.

ABOVE: A CERTAIN AMOUNT OF CLUTTER IS INEVITABLE IN A CHILD'S ROOM. ALLOWING THEM TO DISPLAY THEIR FAVOURITE THINGS WILL ENCOURAGE THEIR GROWING SENSE OF IDENTITY.

LEFT: MOBILES AND HANGING DISPLAYS ARE APPEALING FOR ALL AGES. MUSICAL MOBILES ARE ESPECIALLY SOOTHING FOR BABIES.

Continued

Display

Wonder walls

- Displays are easier to change and cause less damage to underlying surfaces if you create a dedicated area where pictures, photos, postcards and other ephemera can be readily pinned up or taken down. The standard solution is to provide your child with a notice-board or cork board.
- If a noticeboard does not offer enough space, you could think about covering an entire wall with cork tiles or creating a large-scale peg-board where items can be suspended.
- A similar idea is to paint a generous section of wall with blackboard paint where children can scribble away with coloured chalks.

- Magnetic paint will turn a wall surface into the equivalent of a fridge door. The magnetic paint goes on as an undercoat and you can decorate on top with a colour of your choosing.
- A favourite image or snapshot can be blown up to poster size and beyond using digital printing technology. The larger the image will be blown up, the better quality it needs to be: in the case of a digital image, no less than 300dpi (dots per square inch).
- It is easy to create theme walls by making a collage of pictures from magazines or by papering a wall with a collection of maps.
- Cover the ceiling with glow-in-the-dark stars for a magical effect at bedtime.

ABOVE: THESE CIRCULAR FELTBOARDS PROVIDE
PERFECT PLACES TO DISPLAY SNAPSHOTS AND
COMPLEMENT THE SPIRAL WALL-MOUNTED BOOKSHELF.

RIGHT: NOTICEBOARDS, THE BIGGER THE BETTER,
ALLOW CHILDREN TO PIN UP WHATEVER CATCHES THEIR
EYE. THIS ONE INTRODUCES A VIVID SPLASH OF RED.

Index

Acknowledgements

The publisher would like to thank mainstreamimages for their kind permission to reproduce the following photographs:

2 Ray Main/michaelisboyd.com; 6 Ray Main; 10 Darren Chung; 11 Darren Chung/the-englishstudio.com; 12 Sarah Hogan; 13 Darren Chung; 16 Ray Main/Design: Trine Miller; 17 Ray Main; 18 Ray Main; 19 Ray Main/Architect David Wolf; 20 Ray Main; 21 Sarah Hogan/suewilliamsacourt.co.uk; 22 Ray Main/cullumnightingale.com; 23 Ray Main; 24 Ray Main/studioohm.com; 25 Darren Chung; 26 Darren Chung/rehabinteriors.com; 27 Ray Main; 28 Darren Chung/teedinteriors.com; 29 Ray Main/lasdun.com; 30 Paul Raeside; 31 Paul Raeside; 32 Paul Raeside; 33 Ray Main; 34 Darren Chung/meltchocolates.com; 35 Ray Main/Michaelis Boyd Ass Arch; 36 Paul Massey; 37 Darren Chung/teedinteriors.com; 38 Ray Main/ Architect: Polescuk Architects; 39 Ray Main/Adrian and An Jo Mibus; 40 Ray Main/michaelisboyd.com; 41 Ray Main; 42 Darren Chung; 43 Ray Main; 46 Ray Main; 47 Ray Main/JohnDove; 48 Ray Main/Aspen+Brown.com; 49 Ray Main/Gharani Strok; 50 Ray Main/Architect: Laurie Chetwood; 51 Darren Chung/teedinteriors.com; 52 Ray Main/centimetro.net; 53 Ray Main; 54 Ray Main; 55 Darren Chung/teedinteriors.com; 56 Darren Chung/w2products.com; 57 Philip Bier/Bertrand Stillwell; 58 Paul Massey; 59 Darren Chung; 60 Darren Chung; 61 Darren Chung/bobbyopen.com; 62 Ray Main/Taylor Howes Designs Ltd; 63 Ray Main; 64 Ray Main/Nico Rensch Arch; 65 Ray Main/studioohm.com; 66 Ray Main; 67 Paul Massey; 68 Darren Chung/bygraziela.com; 69 Ray Main/Architect: Francesco Draisci; 70 Ray Main; 71 Ray Main/Designer: Claire Nash; 72 Ray Main; 73 Ray Main; 74 Ray Main/blonstein.co.uk; 75 Ray Main/centimetro.net; 78 Darren Chung; 79 Darren Chung/bygraziela.com; 80 Ray Main/Barratta Design; 81 Ray Main; 82 Paul Massey; 83 Ray Main/Architect Peter Wadley; 84 Darren Chung; 85 Ray Main/ Architect: Polescuk Architects; 86 Ray Main/Designer: Ann Von Schewen; 87 Paul Massey; 88 Paul Massey; 89 Ray Main; 90 Ray Main; 91 Ray Main; 92 Paul Raeside; 93 Darren Chung; 94 Darren Chung/newgateclocks.com; 95 Ray Main/michaelisboyd.com; 96 Ray Main/ Architect: Polescuk Architects; 97 Paul Raeside; 98 Ray Main/studioohm.com; 99 Ray Main; 100 Ray Main; 101 Ray Main; 102 Ray Main; 103 Paul Massey; 104 Darren Chung/the-englishstudio.com; 105 Ray Main; 106 Ray Main; 107 Darren Chung/meltchocolates.com; 108 Edmund Sumner/Edward Hill Partnership; 109 Darren Chung/bygraziela.com

We apologise in advance for any unintentional omissions and would be pleased to insert the appropriate acknowledgement in any subsequent publication.

First published in 2011 by Conran Octopus Ltd
a part of Octopus Publishing Group
Endeavour House, 189 Shaftesbury Avenue
London WC2H 8JY
www.octopusbooks.co.uk

A Hachette UK Company
www.hachette.co.uk

Distributed in the United States and Canada by Hachette Book Group USA, 237 Park Avenue New York, NY 10017 USA

Text copyright © Conran Octopus Ltd 2011
Design and layout copyright © Conran Octopus Ltd 2011

The right of Terence Conran to be identified as the Author of this work has been asserted by him in accordance with the Copyright, Designs and Patents Act 1988.

All rights reserved. No part of this book may be reproduced, stored in a retrieval system, or transmitted, in any form or by any means, electronic, electrostatic, magnetic tape, mechanical, photocopying, recording or otherwise, without the prior permission in writing of the Publisher.

British Library Cataloguing-in-Publication Data. A catalogue record for this book is available from the British Library.

Consultant Editor: Elizabeth Wilhide

Publisher: Lorraine Dickey
Managing Editor: Sybella Marlow
Editor: Bridget Ross

Art Director: Jonathan Christie
Picture Researcher: Liz Boyd

Production Manager: Katherine Hockley

ISBN: 978 1 84091 568 6
Printed in China